CW00329611

BRITAIN IN OLD PHOTOGRAPHS

MERTON, MORDEN & MITCHAM

PATRICK LOOBEY

SUTTON PUBLISHING LIMITED

Sutton Publishing Limited
Phoenix Mill · Thrupp · Stroud
Gloucestershire · GL5 2BU

First published 1996

Front cover: Mitcham fair, 1923. Back cover: The Pond, John Innes Park, Merton, *c.* 1914.

British Library Cataloguing in Publication Data
A catalogue record for this book is available from the British Library.

ISBN 0-7509-1124-7

Typeset in 10/12 Perpetua.
Typesetting and origination by
Sutton Publishing Limited.
Printed in Great Britain by
Ebenezer Baylis, Worcester.

PATRICK LOOBEY, born in 1947, has lived in Balham, Putney, Southfields and Streatham. He joined the Wandsworth Historical Society (founded 1953) in 1969 and has served on its archaeological, publishing and management committees, being chairman of the society from 1991 to 1994. Having collected Edwardian postcards of the London area for more than twenty years, he has a wide-ranging collection (20,000 cards plus) encompassing many local roads and subjects. Since 1991, Patrick has compiled a series of photographic histories of Wandsworth, Battersea, Wandsworth & Battersea at War, Balham & Tooting, Streatham, Barnes & Mortlake, Wimbledon and Putney & Roehampton.

ACKNOWLEDGEMENTS

I must thank John Gent for the loan of the following photographs (page numbers: T=Top, L=Lower): 6T, 19T, 30L, 43, 44T, 45T, 46, 47, 48, 49, 50, 51, 52T, 55, 56, 60L, 61T, 63T, 67T, 70L, 77T, 78, 79L, 81, 85T, 98L, 99, 104T, 105T, 107, 108T, 120L, 126L. All the other photographs are taken from the author's collection.

Reproductions of all the views in this book are available from:

P. J. Loobey,
231 Mitcham Lane, Streatham,
London SW16 6PY
(0181-769 0072)

CONTENTS

The Jubilee Clock, the Fair Green, Mitcham, *c.* 1935.

INTRODUCTION

The views within this book capture many of the changes that have occurred within Merton, Morden and Mitcham over the centuries, although all the photographs were taken in the early 1900s. These three villages were bound together by their position on the River Wandle, once the hardest worked river, for its size, in England. Mitcham has archaeological as well as historical evidence as far back as Saxon times. Mills on the Wandle are mentioned as early as AD 1086 in the Domesday Book and, although rebuilt and enlarged over the intervening years, many of these mills were still operating up to the 1960s and '70s.

Merton's medieval priory was of national importance and after the dissolution of the monasteries large country houses and estates were built, and among the most well-known occupants of Merton property was the Admiral Lord Nelson.

The late Victorian period saw many of these country estates broken up for house building and the construction of side roads. Merton Park was developed in the mid-1920s together with Morden; the main spur to the increase in house building was the extension of the Northern Line of the underground railway in 1926. Many large tracts of land were saved as parkland for future generations to enjoy, such as Wandle Bank Park, Ravensbury Park, John Innes Recreation Ground and Morden Hall Park.

Mitcham was on an important coaching route into Surrey and many of the inns survive from the eighteenth century or have origins from those times. The country retreats of many city gentlemen were built here in the seventeenth and eighteenth centuries, the air of Surrey being thought benevolent. Agriculture in the early nineteenth century included the cultivation of lavender and herbs and collecting watercress and willows from the River Wandle.

The late nineteenth century saw the development of many paint and varnish works, sweet factories, and firework manufacturers along the Wandle near Phipps Bridge. Mitcham also saw a building boom in the 1920s, but many of the larger factories were closed in the 1960s and '70s. This resulted in more land being released for housing development.

It is regrettable that more of the older buildings in the district could not have been saved, but the area has seen constant change throughout its history. This book aims to record and explain some of these alterations so that the various scenes and buildings can be better understood.

Patrick Loobey
September 1996

The water splash on the River Wandle, on the London Road near the Grove Mill, 8 June 1910.

Old houses, Phipps Bridge Road, *c*. 1912.

SECTION ONE

MERTON

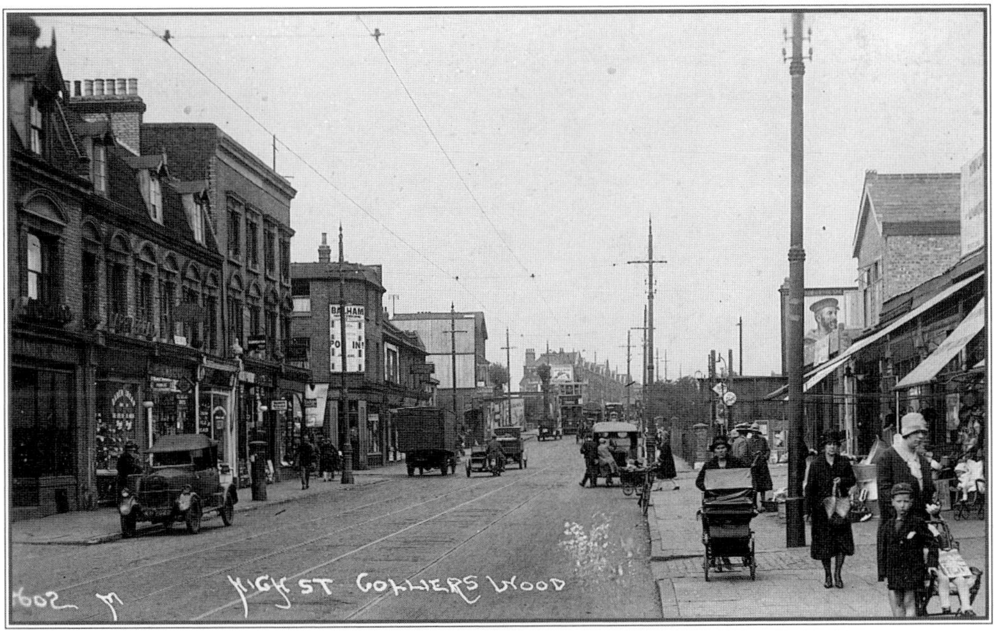

Colliers Wood High Street, c. 1934. The London County Council tram is en route to Wimbledon. Prior to May 1926, the LCC trams terminated in Tooting High Street near Longley Road and passengers had to transfer on to a London United Tramway Co. tramcar whose terminus was not joined to the LCC's. On the left at no. 28 is the pharmacy of Hampden Classey. Enderby Downham Dairy is at no. 32 and Charles Hayes' stationer's and post office at no. 36.

Colliers Wood High Street, *c.* 1912. To the left of Charles Hayes's post office is the depot of the Far Famed Cake Co., at no. 38, with one of their delivery carts waiting outside.

Devonshire Road, *c.* 1912. This area was mainly residential and among the larger properties were St Aubins, Islay and Fairview, nos 24 to 28; Clovelly at no. 48, Ivydene at no. 68, Devonia at no. 72, Trowbury at no. 74, Whitton at no. 76. On the north side of Devonshire Road West was the South Tooting Football Club ground. Several shops were listed before the First World War – Roger Seculer, greengrocer, was situated at no. 18, Edward Gilham, baker, at no. 20, a dairy, confectioner's and greengrocers at no. 119 (which soon became the builder's yard of J.J. Hann) and the dairy of James Robert Cuming at no. 35.

Marlborough Road, *c.* 1912. In 1915 the three Gough sisters lived at no. 8. Miss S. Gough traded as a dressmaker, Miss M. Gough was a teacher of music but it is not known what Miss E. Gough did. The street was otherwise entirely residential except for Mr John Jones whose upholstery business was in premises next to no. 1. The cast iron railings were removed during 1941–2 to assist in the manufacture of munitions.

Wilton Road, *c.* 1918. The two little girls on the right are walking out of Norfolk Road. House names at the time were very similar to those in nearby streets – Brackenhurst at no. 2, Rosslyn at no. 6, St Ives at no. 29 and Dunhelm at no. 31.

High Street Colliers Wood, *c.* 1930. The City and South London Railway Co. extended the underground railway from Clapham to Morden between 1923 and 1926, opening on 13 September 1926. Many of the stations on this southern section of the Northern Line were built to a similar design by Charles Holden, who also designed the familiar logo of London Transport, the circle and bar, as seen outside Colliers Wood station above. The Royal Standard public house is on the left, behind the tram trolley pole. Trades listed before the First World War in this area of the High Street were a harness maker, blind maker, oilman and an incandescent gas fittings dealer. These trades have mostly been superseded by others.

The Royal Six Bells, High Street Colliers Wood, *c.* 1922. This was given the 'Royal' after Edward VII, as Prince of Wales, regularly stopped here for refreshment on his way to Epsom racecourse on Derby Day. The old line of the Roman Stane ('Stane' means stone) Street from Chichester to London is lost at this point until it reappears in Morden. The modern road follows the Roman road from London Bridge to this vicinity almost without deviation.

North Gardens, above, and South Gardens, below, both look clean and fresh in the early 1930s, soon after this post-First World War development had been completed. Britain was the first country in the world to have an electricity supply national grid and large metal pylons were erected across the country during the 1920s. One of these pylons an be seen behind North Gardens.

High Street, Merton, *c.* 1914. The London and General Omnibus bus garage, opened in November 1913, is seen next to The Old King's Head public house.

High Street, Merton, mid-1920s. The London and General Omnibus bus garage has been extended and widened since the top photograph was taken. A young boy attempts to sail his boat in the River Wandle, watched by waiting bus passengers and a bus driver.

Merton High Street, *c.* 1910. The Old King's Head public house is on the left and further on is The Royal Six Bells public house. The factorys and mills on the right have been replaced by the entrance to a large supermarket called Savacentre.

The Old King's Head public house, seen here *c.* 1908, has a questionable date of 1496 on the front wall. Young & Co. substantially rebuilt and enlarged the pub in 1931 and it is now just called The King's Head.

Wandle Park, *c.* 1907. The rustic bridge over the Pickle Ditch as it flowed through the park. Mrs Richardson Evans of Wimbledon presented the Wandle Park mill pond to the National Trust in December 1905 in memory of her brother, John Feeney, proprieter of the *Birmingham Post* and *Mail*, who had died eighteen months previously.

Wandle Bank House, *c.* 1907. From 1791 to 1821 this was the home of James Perry, editor and proprieter of the *Morning Chronicle*, founded in 1770. James Perry was also proprieter of the nearby Merton Corn Mill, erected in about 1800, that was later used by Connolly's Leather Ltd. The 10 acres of parkland including the house were secured by Wimbledon Corporation to save it from development. The land had belonged to Mrs Ashby, who had recommended the setting out of recreation grounds in Wimbledon and Merton. The park was opened on Thursday 13 July 1907 by HRH Princess Louise, Duchess of Argyll. The Duke of Argyll and the Bishop of Kingston also attended. D Squadron of the Surrey Imperial Yeomanry attended on arrival at Wimbledon village and provided an escort to the park. Eighty-one small plots were set aside in the park for local schools so that pupils could grow seeds and plants. Wandle Bank House was demolished in the 1970s and replaced by a block of flats called Kendall Court, an extension of the flat conversion at Connolly's Mill alongside. The park now has two very large electricity pylons standing within it and the Pickle Ditch is strewn with rubbish and the water stagnant.

High Street, Merton, *c.* 1936. To the right of the bus on the corner of Abbey Road is The Nelson public house which has a number of tiled panels on the outside walls depicting scenes of Admiral Nelson's life and his flagship HMS *Victory*. By the time this photograph was taken the motor car was increasing in numbers but certainly not enough to choke the major local roads.

High Street, Merton, *c.* 1922. The Horse and Groom public house on the right survives as do the shops on the left on the corner of Merton Road. The shops on the right were soon to be demolished for the construction of South Wimbledon tube station.

The old gateway of the priory at Merton, *c.* 1910. This is all that now survives (except for some remains on view below Merantun Way) of the twelfth-century priory founded by Augustinian Canons in 1117. The monastery was where Henry VI was crowned in 1437 and where Thomas à Becket was educated as a youth. The priory was surrendered at the dissolution of the monasteries in 1538 and the stone was soon sold off; some of it was taken as far as Battersea but the majority was used to build Nonsuch Palace at Cheam.

Corfield Ltd factory alongside the Wandle at Merton, *c.* 1930. The factory specialized in press steel work and deep metal stampings. They also manufactured holloware and aluminium domestic utensils. The Wandle is on the right and passes under Merton High Street and reappears to the left of Wandle Bank Park. The Royal Six Bells public house is on the extreme right. Merton Board Mills stood the other side of the factory on the High Street side. Merton Abbey station, which is visible in the foreground, has now been rebuilt as Merantuń Way . The factory site is now the shopping area called Savacentre.

The Gatehouse, or Abbey House, was built in the early eighteenth century and stood on the south side of Merton High Street, where Mill Road and Croft Road were built. The Smith family lived here at the beginning of the nineteenth century and gave hospitality to Emma Hamilton in 1808 when Merton Park, Nelson's home nearby, was sold off. The widow of Captain Cook lived here for some years. The house was demolished in about 1907. The photograph below shows the house being demolished.

South Wimbledon tube station, *c*. 1936. The Horse and Groom public house was left untouched when the tube station was built in 1926, but the cottages and shops at what had been called Eliza Place had to be demolished. The station is misnamed as this is Merton rather than Wimbledon, but railway companies have always been a law unto themselves when naming their stations.

The Grove Hotel, corner of Morden Road and Kingston Road, *c*. 1907. The title 'hotel' was used as accommodation was provided together with a new supply of horses in this mid-nineteenth-century pub, which was demolished and rebuilt in 1912. The pub is now called The Grove Tavern.

Watery Lane, *c.* 1912. Manor Gardens is to the right, just beyond the two ladies. The view is from Kingston Road; the two properties on the right were named Harptree and Frensham.

Merton Rush, *c.* 1910. This small triangle of properties where Watery Lane meets Kingston Road consisted of a number of small eighteenth-century properties, among them The Old Leather Bottle public house. In 1898, when a new building further along Kingston Road was built, the pub was converted into a shop, seen in the background as the Copus greengrocers. The shop on the left corner, behind the large tree, was the Morden Hall Farm Dairy.

The Nelson Hospital, Kingston Road, *c.* 1918. This is the private entrance to the nurses' home at the hospital, which was built in 1911 and opened the following year. The hospital cost £32,000 to build and the Borough of Merton added a new wing in 1922 to commemorate the men of Merton who fell during the First World War.

The Masonic hall, 76–8 Kingston Road, *c.* 1905; it was opened in 1900. The hall was paid for by John Innes and hosted concerts given by the Merton boys club as well as being available for public hire. The hall was converted for use as the local library in 1933. In 1942 it reverted to its original use.

The council offices, 116–8, Kingston Road, *c.* 1912. Merton parish council erected these offices in 1900. They were enlarged over the years. Between 1894 and 1907 Merton was administered by Croydon Urban District Council and in 1907 Merton UDC was formed. Attached to the council offices was the local fire station, seen on the left.

Aerial view of William Harland & Son Ltd works at Phipps Bridge Road, *c.* 1930. The company was founded in the 1820s and manufactured paints, enamels, varnishes, cellulose and synthetic finishes. The factory occupied a large site between Phipps Bridge Road and Church Road, with the works entrance in Aberdeen Road. The factory closed in the 1960s and was sold off for development in 1967. Houses in Brangwyn Crescent were erected on the site in the 1970s and ’80s.

Rutlish School, Kingston Road, *c.* 1910. William Rutlish, in his will of 1687, left £400 for apprenticing poor children. The sum had grown considerably over the years to almost £6,000 and it was decided in 1894 to erect a science school in Merton, guided mainly by the thoughts of John Innes. The school was opened in September 1895 and survived until the 1970s when it was demolished, being considered too small for a modern school. Station Road is on the right.

The gymnasium, Rutlish School, *c.* 1920. It was equipped with the then modern Swedish drill apparatus.

Rutlish School, *c.* 1920. The long ladder on the wall was probably a fire safety requirement of the local authority. The school offered a number of educational courses in addition to teaching science. The school had room for 250 boys. It included 14 class rooms, a large art room, physical and chemical laboratories, a lecture room, manual training workshop and rooms for the headmaster and governors.

St Mary's Parish Church, Merton, *c*. 1914. First mentioned in the Domesday Book of 1086, a church has stood on this site since late Saxon times. Rebuilt in about 1115 by the Norman knight Gilbert, the church has been altered and enlarged many times since. There are many monuments in the church to local notable people – Lord Nelson, John Innes and William Rutlish. Also on display are some stone mouldings from the 1921 excavations at Merton Priory and a Norman arch, which, having been recovered from the priory, was re-erected here.

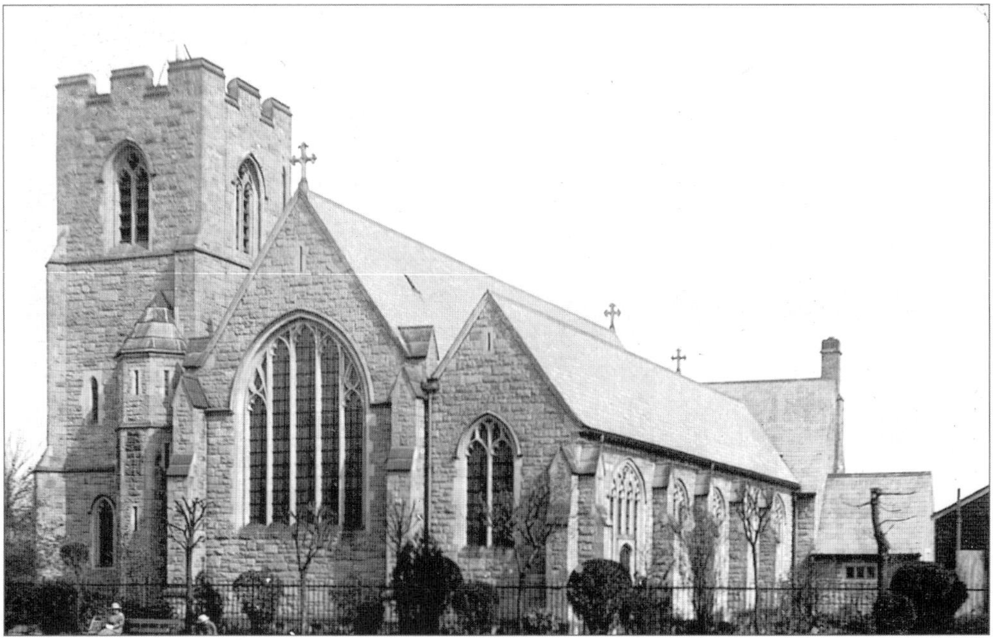

St John the Devine Church, *c*. 1914. The church was built at a cost of £11,000 in order to ease the pressure on the parish church. It could seat 550 people and was consecrated on 31 October 1914.

SECTION TWO

MERTON PARK

Merton Park level crossing, Kingston Road, c. 1910. Since 1855 this level crossing has halted traffic along Kingston Road with the arrival of each train. However, it prevented the need for the construction of a road bridge and the demolition of The White Hart public house on the other side of the signal box. This issue was discussed frequently by Merton Council and the Southern Railway during the 1920s and '30s. The White Hart public house was badly damaged by bombing during the Second World War and rebuilt in the 1950s. It has recently been converted into an Irish theme pub called Bodhrans Barneys.

Merton Park station, *c.* 1910. The line was opened in 1857/8 and the station in 1868 and called Lower Merton until 1877 when John Innes, who was developing much of the local area, persuaded the railway company to change the name to Merton Park. Station Road is to the right between the houses, with the Tooting, Merton and Wimbledon line, which closed in the 1960s, to Merton Abbey below. The Croydon line is to the left and the signal box at the level crossing is towards the centre in the distance. In the lower view the station entrance gives the air of a small country halt.

The so-called three bridges at Merton Park station, *c.* 1900. These were erected to gain access to the platforms of both the Croydon and Tooting lines. With the removal of the Tooting line in the 1960s only the length of bridge near Dorset Road survives.

The house of Our Lady, Merton Park, *c.* 1920. This was one of many seventeenth- and eighteenth-century cottages which survived into the early twentieth century only to be demolished as modern development has expanded across the landscape.

Cannon Hill Lane, *c.* 1907.

Cannon Hill Lane, *c.* 1926. A five-barred gate was in place to prevent sheep and other animals straying from their fields. The lane was a quiet country road up to the 1930s.

Cannon Hill Farm, *c.* 1914. This farm stood next to the Merton Urban District Council allotments and the farmer in 1914 was Walter Smith. The farm is a reminder that Merton Park was a rural area until relatively recently, development only beginning in the twentieth century. Even as late as the 1920s there was much open land as far as Sutton.

The new houses in Cannon Hill Lane, *c.* 1936, seen from the lake on the common. The second phase of house building by Merton and Morden UDC in Cannon Lane, beyond Martin Way, was started in 1927.

Cannon Hill Lane, *c.* 1936. Residential developments such as this one continued to blur the distinction between the countryside and the suburb. In the distance, beyond the telegraph pole, is the newly built Barclays Bank.

Development of Merton Park, seen from the air, 1923. Fields surround the building of the Whatley Estate. The central circle of houses is Mawson Close and the larger road from top to bottom is Whatley Avenue. The John Innes Recreation Ground is to the bottom of this view. The main contractor was J.W. Ellingham of Dartford, Kent, working for the local district council. The area was previously called Bushey Mead.

Abbot Avenue, *c.* 1926. The houses are in 'as new' condition but the roadway is unmetalled. The local authority would have to send a water cart along to dampen the road surface to contain the dust.

Aylward Road is seen in the late 1920s or early 1930s, with newly planted trees lining the pavement. The fashion at the time was to leave a small grass verge on the kerbside as compensation for the loss of countryside.

Botsford Road, *c.* 1926. At the far end of the road is Raynes Park School, built in 1909. Until the mid-1920s access to the school was along Botsford Road, which remained unmade. The houses are now complete and occupied in this view.

Burstow Road, *c.* 1930. Besides planting the roadside trees, the developers did manage to preserve some of the older trees which can be seen above the roof line.

Chatsworth Avenue, *c.* 1914. The earlier developments in Merton Park are more pleasing to the eye and the houses more decorative – notice the attractive, pierced barge-boards on the gables and railings on the garden walls.

Church Lane, Merton, *c.* 1910. The lane, off Mostyn Road, leads to the parish church of St Mary. The elm trees were a major feature.

Cliveden Road, *c.* 1914. Children could play in some safety in the middle of the road without disturbance or much danger from passing traffic. The iron hoop carried by the little boy nearest the camera was a favourite toy before the First World War but could cause some fireworks if dropped into the roadway slot of the LCC tramways.

Dorset Road, *c.* 1914. Two little girls can wander along the tree-lined road in perfect safety – most passing traffic would have only attained a speed of 4 or 5 mph. The road was laid out by John Innes as an early part of his development scheme for the area and his architect, H.G. Quartermain, lived here in a house called Abingdon. Other houses were called Faircroft, Allandene, Ellangowan, Montrose and Lynedoch. An office of the Merton Park Estate Co. was situated on the east side of the road.

John Innes Park, 1914. John Innes acquired the Merton Park Estate in 1867 specifically to develop it for housing. He was wise enough to leave several large open spaces as parks and the John Innes Park, off Watery Lane, was endowed with many plants and bushes together with an ornamental pond and fountain. It was opened on 12 July 1909, some years after his death.

Haynt Walk, Merton Park on the Whatley Estate, *c.* 1925. It was given this name after an old wood that stood here and a line of these trees, probably an old boundary line, is apparent in these views. The writer of the above postcard explained that in July 1925 it took 1½ hours to reach Merton Park on a bus from King's Cross at a cost of 9 *d* for the whole journey.

Kingswood Road, Merton Park, *c*. 1925. A man sweeping the gutter in the far distance is the only activity in this scene.

Manor Gardens, *c*. 1930. The road name alludes to the manor house erected by John Innes from 1868 on the site of nearby Manor Farm in Watery Lane.

Mayfield Road, *c.* 1925. The road names chosen for Merton Park were meant to reflect the countryside which had once covered this area.

Merton Hall Road, *c.* 1925. The interesting feature of these properties is the terracotta griffins on the pinnacles of the front gables. Harold Granville Barnard, solicitor and commissioner for oaths, lived at no. 93. Stevenson and Rush, a provisions store and post office, was situated at no. 156 and J.H. Martin, photographic film manufacturers, was at no. 142.

Melbourne Road, *c.* 1910. With a school leaving age of fourteen, many young boys found work delivering items for local domestic and grocery stores. The boy on the right has a wicker basket on a two-wheeled trolley.

Kingston Road, Merton Park, *c.* 1914. Mostyn Road is on the right. The large house on the left is called The Look Out and is on the corner of Wilton Crescent, at 217 Kingston Road. It was built in 1886 and was once the home of George Hadfield, proprieter of the large paint manufacturer Hadfields Ltd of Mitcham. It is now used by St Christopher's Fellowship, founded in 1870 to assist young people in difficulties.

Oxford Avenue, *c*. 1925. Why the photographer would want to wait until everyone had disappeared from view is rather strange as even his own bicycle would lend some scale or interest to the scene. The Cromwell Engineering Co. operated from premises at no. 81.

Mostyn Road, *c*. 1910. When John Innes was developing this road he chose chestnut trees to line it. The larger houses were named Bolingbroke, The Limes, Crowsteps, The Red House etc. The road was originally laid out in Victorian times only as far as Church Path from the Kingston Road. The rest of the houses were added in the 1930s. Two members of Merton and Morden UDC lived here in the 1920s – Benjamin T. King at Lemsford and the Revd W. James Mackain at Aubrey Lodge.

Richmond Avenue, *c.* 1924. During the 1920s Merton Park Maternity Home was located at no. 14, with Miss A.E. Howe as midwife. This scene was transformed on 20 September 1940, when a German Junkers bomber crashed on to nos 2 and 4, with several of the crew being killed.

Sheridan Road, *c.* 1910. The one regular delivery to each road was the horse-drawn dairy cart, arriving three and four times a day in the period before refrigerators were commonplace. In 1915 Col. Edward Charles Stanton lived at Allington Lodge. The other unnumbered houses were called Penshurst, Heathfield and Hollybroke. By 1920 Edenhurst was numbered 7, where Isaac Mawson Brash, councillor of Merton and Morden UDC, lived.

Wilton Crescent, *c.* 1924. Lt. Col William R. Thomas lived at no. 12 in 1915.

Wilton Grove, *c.* 1924. At this time the Wilton Lawn Tennis Club was situated at no. 26, next to Henfield Road. Alfred J. Dearberg was secretary to the club.

SECTION THREE

MORDEN

Morden station, c. 1930. The greatest spur to development in the area was the opening of the Northern Line of the London Underground railway on 13 September 1926. The station, designed by Charles Holden, incorporated a shopping arcade with a ladies' hairdressers, a branch of the Midland Bank and also a Belgravia Chocolate Company shop. A three-storey office block above the shops and station has been built called Athena House.

Central Road, Morden village, *c.* 1920. On the right is The Plough public house, on the left is the rectory and two houses called The Laurels and Hazelwood.

The Plough public house, *c.* 1915, advertised good accommodation for cyclists and could supply teas. The village post office on the left was run by Miss Fannie Adams. The pub was demolished in the early 1930s and was replaced by The Morden Tavern on the other side of the road.

The Plough public house and Morden village post office, *c.* 1920. The village 'bobby' looks on, no doubt untroubled by too many crime waves in this area.

The George Inn, Epsom Road, *c.* 1905. Possibly dating back to the sixteenth century, The George Inn was dependent on passing trade for its livelihood. The large sign beyond the pub advertises 'Thorley's gruel for horses' and suggests the traveller should 'Stop here for a refresher for your nag'. The pub is still called The George Inn and is now a Harvester restaurant and hotel.

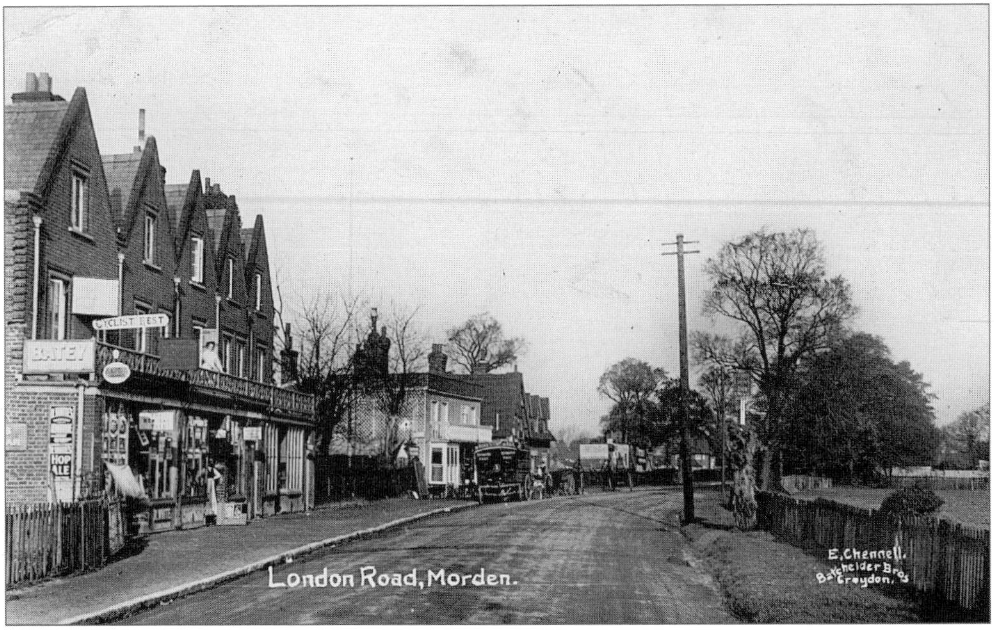

London Road, Morden, *c.* 1910. The first stop on the left was the Frank Martin Dining Rooms and cyclist's rest and next to it was Ernest Chennell's grocery and post office. The furniture van is standing outside The Crown public house, demolished in the 1960s when a new Crown pub was constructed as part of the Crown House office development on this site.

London Road, Morden, *c.* 1910. Within twenty years all of these fields and trees were covered over by modern Morden.

London Road, central Morden, *c.* 1949. The buses are wartime issue, a basic design intended to save on materials and a means of supplying London with buses to replace the many damaged because of wartime bombing. The buses soldiered on for some years after the war. The Northern Line Underground station is to the left of the no. 156 bus on the left.

London Road, Morden, *c.* 1949. The three-storey Co-op store was completed in 1940, replacing the eight-year-old store. The austerity of the postwar years is displayed in the age of the vehicles, which all date from the late 1930s.

Morden Hall Road, *c.* 1910. The Telegraph messenger boy, who delivered telegrams, with his bicycle has the whole road to himself. Morden Hall Park is to the left.

Epsom Road, *c.* 1910. Farmland on both sides of the road greeted the visitor to Morden up to the mid-1920s. Part of these fields were later to become Morden Park.

The original caption to this photograph, *c.* 1910, proclaims the scene as at the top of George Hill. Epsom Road is to the right, with the old school house. Central Road is to the left and London Road is off to the right behind the cameraman. The small single storey-building behind the wooden fence was yet another cyclists' rest, providing teas. This junction was altered dramatically in the 1970s by road widening schemes and the cottage on the left was demolished.

George Hill on the Epsom Road, *c.* 1910, on the approach to Morden.

Morden Hall Farm, Morden Road, *c*. 1905. The motor car showroom of Mann Egerton now stands here. The farm was bought by John Innes in the 1860s and was in use as a dairy from the 1890s until the late 1920s. The dairy carts would leave this farm building as often as four times a day on their local rounds. The farm was demolished in 1930.

Morden Hall Farm, *c.* 1905. The farm and the animals kept were of great interest to John Innes. He ensured that the latest equipment was used, and took pleasure and pride in the pigs which won many prizes. Four of the farm horses were used to draw the farm wagon that carried John Innes' coffin for burial at St Mary's Parish Church, Merton on 12 August 1904.

Ravensbury Mill on the River Wandle, *c.* 1920. The Morden road crosses here. This early nineteenth-century mill was used by the Rutter family which manufactured tobacco products here, chiefly the well-known Mitcham Shag tobacco. The sports equipment firm of Whiteleys used the mill from 1925 to 1980, when it fell into disuse. The main mill buildings were converted in 1995/6 for private accommodation.

Morden Cinema, a few months after it opened on 8 December 1932. The films *Cynara* and *Gabriel over the White House* were showing. The cinema also incorporated a café for patrons. In 1937 it was renamed the Odeon and finally closed on 13 January 1973. The building was in use as a DIY store, but has since been demolished and shops and flats now occupy the site.

Mr Conroy outside his confectionery shop with a party of schoolchildren in Central Road next to the old parish hall, *c.* 1933. Originally this building was a school that opened in 1731 on the strength of a £300 bequest made by a daughter of George Garth; it was enlarged in 1872 and 1889. In 1910 the school became the parish hall.

Garendon Road, St Helier, Morden, *c.* 1933. Developed by the LCC, the estate was named in honour of the LCC Alderman Lady St Helier, who promoted improved housing conditions in the London region.

Green Lane South, *c.* 1933. The LCC purchased 825 acres of land in Morden and Sutton after the First World War mainly during the late 1920s. The bulk of the construction work took place between 1930 and 1937 and by 1939 there were 9,000 dwellings and a population of 40,000 people. A few more properties were added after the Second World War.

Hyde Walk, St Helier, *c.* 1933.

SECTION FOUR

MITCHAM

Mitcham Common, c. 1908. At the end of the nineteenth century the common was an open prairie of grass and gorse interspersed with various bog holes, water-filled ditches and diggings. The few trees in this view surround the Ravensbury Arms public house. The original eighteenth-century inn is against the roadway on the left of the group of buildings and the 1906 replacement pub is slightly to the right of it, behind the second tram pole.

The 1906 Ravensbury Arms public house, *c.* 1935. It was well set back from the roadway, no doubt hoping to entice passing traffic to pull in and refresh the drivers as well as the horses.

The Ravensbury Arms public house, Mitcham Common, *c.* 1903. This eighteenth-century pub had chickens roaming in the roadway in front of the doorway. The carrier's cart gives the scene the look more of a farmyard than of a halt on the road to Croydon.

Mitcham Common, *c.* 1914, at the junction of Croydon Road and Carshalton Road, which leads off to Mitcham Junction station.

The ladies' clubhouse at Princes Golf Club on Mitcham Common, near Mitcham Junction railway station, *c.* 1914. The clubhouse was situated on the west of the railway line and a rustic bridge was provided to allow access to the golf course on the east of the tracks. The ladies' clubhouse has now gone and the ladies relocated to some simple changing rooms in the main clubhouse. Each Tuesday is designated Ladies' Day on the course.

Mitcham Junction railway station, *c*. 1914. The station was opened in 1868 and was some distance from the village of Mitcham. This fact meant it did not influence the housing and commercial development of the area, as central railway stations tended to do. The station master, probably Mr Andrea Holdaway, is standing on the platform edge. In the distance is the ladies' clubhouse on the right and the main golf clubhouse to the left of the station.

Mitcham Junction railway station, *c*. 1912.

Mill Green flats, off London Road near Mitcham Junction, *c.* 1955. This early high-rise postwar housing development was erected by Mitcham Council.

The Windmill public house, *c.* 1914. This pub was situated on Commonside West and was erected in about 1870 on the site of an earlier beer house which dated back to at least 1846. The eighteenth-century windmill stood some 100 yards away and was of the horizontal type where a series of shutters on the exterior walls were opened to allow the wind to drive the internal horizontal vanes. The eighteenth-century weatherboarded cottages were destroyed by enemy action during the Second World War and the site is now occupied by 2157 (Mitcham) Squadron Air Training Corp.

Mitcham Common, *c.* 1910. Both scenes depict the water ditches and small lagoons that dotted the common. In the lower view are some of the trees planted by unemployed people taking part in a scheme run by Mitcham Council to provide temporary employment for those seeking work. The local authority ruined the common in the 1940s and '50s by dumping refuse there to fill in the many lagoons and many local people demonstrated to try and halt the dust carts.

Gypsies on Mitcham Common, *c.* 1904. Many gypsies were attracted to Mitcham each August with the staging of the annual Mitcham fair. They would stay for the harvesting of lavender and knock at local houses selling clothes-pegs, rush mats, bags and besom brooms.

Mitcham Common with The Three Kings public house, *c.* 1925.

The Beehive bridge, *c.* 1914. The bridge is named after The Beehive public house, the white painted building on the right. Notice the pools of water on the badly drained common.

The Beehive bridge, *c.* 1953. Different modes of transport are seen in this view of the bridge and the wooden railings seen in the top view have been replaced with a metal fence. Wartime air raid shelters are seen to the left of the road on the common.

The Three Kings public house, Commonside East, *c.* 1935. The pub was built in mock Tudor style in 1928 and replaced a much smaller eighteenth-century pub of the same name. The pond takes its name from the pub, but was once called the Great Pond.

Three Kings Pond, Mitcham Common, *c.* 1910. The posts in the water were a guide mark for carters who took their vehicles through the water to enable the horses to drink and also to expand and tighten the wooden joints of the wheels. The posts are still in place but the entrance by the two boys has now been blocked by some bollards.

Wilson Cottage Hospital, Cranmer Road, *c.* 1932. The hospital was opened in 1928 with donations made by the building developer Sir Isaac Wilson. The Princess Royal, Princess Mary carried out the opening ceremony. Throughout the 1930s fund-raising activities were enthusiastically attended and the hospital was enlarged in 1934. The 1938 hospital carnival had a cast of 1,500 – 2 bands including the Scots Greys, who put on a mounted display, a parade of Mitcham's champion athletes and 100 ladies of the League of Health and Beauty. There were also famous jockeys riding donkeys, a fancy dress parade with a carnival queen, 18 tableaux, a funfair, sack race and a finale of fireworks.

Vine Cottage, *c.* 1914. In 1912 this house, which stood on the Lower Green West opposite Hall Place, was thought to be the oldest in the parish, probably dating back to the Tudor period. The house was used as a school during the nineteenth century. It was last occupied in about 1890 and, having fallen into disrepair, was demolished. The parish beadle had been a resident and the block of police flats which replaced the cottage was named Beadle Court and Vine Court.

The Wandle at Mitcham, *c.* 1913. Besides being the power source for a number of mills, the waters provided trout and many other fish up to the end of the nineteenth century. The banks of the Wandle at Mitcham would often be used for picnics.

The bridge across the River Wandle on the London Road to Sutton, *c.* 1914. The bridge was rebuilt in brick by the county after 1759, when Morden and Mitcham parishes were admonished for poor maintenance of the old structure. To the right of the bridge was a ford used by carters.

London Road, *c.* 1913. Road widening schemes implemented since the Second World War have meant that all these walls and buildings have disappeared.

Mitcham railway station, *c.* 1914. In 1855 the line from Wimbledon to Croydon was opened. At Mitcham station, for a short distance, the line followed the track of the Surrey Iron Railway, the world's first public railway. The full complement of station staff is on the platform facing the camera and well-tended flower beds on both platforms bring some brightness to what might otherwise be a drab site. In 1915–16 the station master was Walter Henry Martin. The Iron Railway was built in 1801–3 to connect Wandsworth and Croydon and was only used with horse-drawn trucks.

London Road, *c.* 1910. This view is facing towards Mitcham, with The King's Head public house at the far end of the buildings on the right. The three-storey black and white building on the right was the post office. The original caption to the photograph described this section of the road as The Broadway – not an accurate description until the road widening of the 1960s created a four-lane roadway here.

London Road, Mitcham, *c.* 1913. The White Hart public house is on the right and The King's Head public house is on the left on the corner of the Cricket Green. The small round disc mounted on a pole, on the left, states that the speed limit for motor vehicles is 10 mph. The buildings on the left were demolished because of road widening schemes implemented after the Second World War.

The King's Head public house, *c.* 1910. It is located on the corner of London Road and the Cricket Green. The façade of the pub dates from about 1760 while the rear of the building dates back to the seventeenth century. This pub, once an important coaching inn on the route to Epsom, has been renamed The Burn Bullock after a licensée, Burnley Bullock, resident from 1941 to 1954, who was a well-known local cricketer.

London Road, *c.* 1930. The King's Head public house is on the far right corner, just out of view. The White Hart public house is on the left just beyond the delivery van which is parked outside an early BP petrol station with a glass tube advertising sign rising above the front of the building.

London Road, *c.* 1908, top and *c.* 1949, below. The forty years that separate these two views show that improvements barely disguise the basic looks of the local buildings. The obvious change was the loss of The Cricketers pub during wartime bombing (subsequently rebuilt), the decoration added to The White Hart public house and the stone facing to Barclay's bank.

According to the date above the front door, The White Hart was founded in 1768.

The Lower Green East, Mitcham, *c.* 1913, or the Causeway. The tall building, on the right, is the police station and the Cricket Green is on the left, which is now surrounded by some low railings. The single-storey storey building to the right of the horse and cart was the dye works of W. Pugh. The group of buildings on the right, nos 40–46 Cricket Green, still survive.

London Road viewed from the Causeway, *c.* 1928. The King's Head public house is on the left, with Horsley Bros Cricket Green garage alongside and the white stuccoed White Hart public house on the far side of the road. The tram is seen running on the extension into London Road beyond The King's Head. A small horse-drawn tea stall is stationed on the corner of the Cricket Green.

The Causeway, *c.* 1908. This area was raised slightly above the badly drained Cricket Green. The coach and cart works, on the left of the motor car, was the works of G. Hart & Sons, cycle makers, originally a blacksmith's and today is a motor car showroom called Village Cars. The village police station is seen further along, the tallest building in the row. In 1915 the police station had a complement of 7 sergeants, 34 constables and station sergeant William Emson. The police station was rebuilt in 1964.

The Cricket Green, *c.* 1914. Cricket has been played here for over 300 years – the first mention of a game here was in 1685. Mitcham Cricket Club has supplied a number of players for Surrey and also England. There have been various plans to sell off the land for housing development and in the 1930s a road widening scheme threatened to destroy the ground. But the ground has survived and is well-used by many residents of Mitcham.

The Vestry Hall, far right, and The Cricketers public house seen from across the Cricket Green, *c.* 1914. At this time public telephone boxes were unknown and a telephone call box was available for the public in the Vestry Hall.

The Cricketers public house, *c.* 1914. This eighteenth-century inn was the headquarters of Mitcham Cricket Club and in the early days of Australian cricket tours to England the visiting team would train here. The pub was destroyed in September 1940 by a direct hit from a high explosive bomb and the site lay empty, except for two temporary wooden huts, for eighteen years before a replacement pub was built. The London and General bus is en route to Acton Green.

The Vestry House, *c*. 1913. This building was erected in 1887 to hold parish council meetings and as a centre for village activities. The building incorporated a fire station, to the left, which was not superseded until the separate station was erected at the rear of the Vestry House in Lower Green West in 1927. Mitcham's first professional fire officer was only appointed in 1920.

Mitcham Court, *c*. 1914. Mitcham Court, on the right, was previously called Elm Court. Elm Lodge, on the left, dates from 1808 and was occupied in the early nineteenth century by the village doctor, Dr Parrott, and for a short time by the artist Sir William Nicholson. The house has been a doctor's surgery for most of the twentieth century. A milestone on the London Road opposite Elm Lodge still advises that the distance to Whitehall is only 8½ miles. The photographer stood on the Cricket Green and the path seen here now has low railings dividing the grassed areas.

Mitcham war memorial, *c.* 1926. The memorial was dedicated 'To the men of Mitcham who falling, conquered in the Great War 1914–19'. Although the war is recognized as ending on 11 November 1918, the armistice was not formalized until the treaty of Versailles was signed in June 1919, and peace celebrations were held in July. The memorial is smothered in sprays of flowers left by surviving relatives and friends. A plaque was added at the base dedicated 'To the men, women and children who lost their lives in the Second World War'.

The parade of shops in London Road near the Upper or Fair Green, *c.* 1914. One of the first large-scale commercial developments in Mitcham was this shopping parade which included M. Ireland's grocers, Martin Brothers and the 'World Stores'. The horse-drawn delivery van outside Ireland's store is from the baker's, Joys Ltd of Dawes Road, Fulham.

The shopping parade, London Road, *c.* 1949. A wide variety of outlets were housed in this row of shops. On the left is Thomas Francis Ironmongers, at no. 286. He also had a boot and shoe shop at nos 280–2 and a draper's store at no 284, since demolished in a road widening and rebuilding scheme.

The Fair Green, Mitcham, *c.* 1914. The green is to the left and the view is facing north. On the right is W. Turner's bakery and confectioner's shop at 33 Upper Green East.

The Fair Green, Mitcham, *c.* 1914. The green is to the right and in the far distance is London Road shopping parade. The memorial clock was erected in 1898 to celebrate the diamond jubilee of Queen Victoria's reign in 1897. The village pump previously stood on the site. The unveiling ceremony took place on 29 November 1899. The gas lamps have unfortunately been removed.

The Fair Green, Mitcham, *c.* 1926. Lack of traffic and the speed limits imposed within the town made wandering along the roadway on foot a passable means of progress. The tram, heading towards the camera, is bound for the Tooting Junction terminus.

The Fair Green, or Upper Green, *c.* 1914, with a row of eighteenth-century shops on the east side. On the left is Searl's removals and second-hand furniture dealers. The small building next door proclaimed itself 'The Little Wonder Dining Rooms'.

The Fair Green, 1953. The decorations were for the celebration of Queen Elizabeth II's coronation in June 1953.

The Fair Green, 1953. This photograph was probably taken in the autumn after the coronation. The green had been laid out as a small park, but due to neglect and vandalism was altered dramatically in 1993/4 by the local authority. The area was grassed over and the road system changed.

Upper Green West, *c.* 1914, with two more features that have since been removed. On the left is the eighteenth-century Nags Head public house, demolished and rebuilt, but even the rebuild has since been demolished. The bandstand on the apex of the green has also been removed.

Mitcham fair, seen here in 1922, is held over a three-day period in August each year. It is said that the fair dates back to 1559, although this has never been proved. The showmen would take over the centre of the town and normal life and business would come to a standstill.

Showmen's booths and stalls encroach on to the roadway, *c.* 1914. The policeman was on duty to ensure the smooth passage of any passing trams.

The 1908 Mitcham fair. On the right, near The King's Arms public house, is a travelling picture booth displaying 'living pictures'.

In 1911 the children's amusements were priced at 1 *d* a ride. Besides the normal fairground rides there were boxing and wrestling booths, peep shows, displays of dwarfs and a variety of live animals. Food stalls would accompany the fair, offering oysters, pickled salmon, humbugs and much more.

A. Ball & Son's Lyceum picture show at Mitcham fair, 1911. The show was certainly popular with the crowds as a steady stream of people are queuing to the right of the stage. The amusement advertises that the best pictures are on show and that all classes of seats are available for 2 *d* and 3 *d*. Most films at this time only lasted five minutes.

Mitcham fair, *c.* 1908. The young man sitting behind the costermonger's cart is selling lemonade from a beer barrel at ½*d* per glass. It looks like most of the youngsters and young ladies are wearing their Sunday best for the occasion.

Mitcham fair, *c.* 1909. With the coming of the tramway and other increases in traffic the local council wanted the fair removed from the town centre and the last event held on the Fair Green was in 1923. From 1924 Three Kings Piece became the venue for the fair.

The King's Arms public house, on the left, *c.* 1913. Originally this pub was a small timber clapperboard building of the late eighteenth century; it was demolished and rebuilt in its present form in 1899. The Buck's Head public house, on the right, was rebuilt at about the same time as The King's Arms when this narrow part of the road was widened in 1900.

The King's Arms and The Buck's Head, *c.* 1930. Notice the open-top motor coach, or charabanc, outside The Buck's Head, a popular form of touring in the 1920s and '30s. The King's arms displayed on the pub are those of George III.

London Road, *c.* 1907. This part of the road was sometimes referred to as the High Street and had been a bottleneck for some years. The arrival of the tramway system in 1906 gave local people the opportunity of shopping or working in Croydon and Tooting, or even further afield. The road system was altered in 1994 and the High Street was pedestrianised.

The Buck's Head public house, *c.* 1914. This advertising postcard was produced when the proprietor was William H. Poole. The parish vestry meetings were often held in the pub before the Vestry Hall was built in 1887. The pub was renamed The White Lion of Mortimer in 1991.

Mitcham fair, at Three Kings Piece on the common, August 1953. A funfair is also held here each year at the Mitcham May Carnival. A dispute between the organizers of the fair and the local authority regarding the pitch rents led to the fair being cancelled between 1974 and 1983.

Cranmer bridge, *c.* 1914. A solitary horse and cart is crossing the bridge over the railway on an unmetalled road. The trees and bushes have grown substantially since this photograph was taken and now cover the embankments on both sides.

Christ Church, Christchurch Road, *c.* 1913. The area around the church is known as Singlegate and a temporary church was erected here in 1864 to ease congestion at the parish church. The foundation stone for Christ Church was laid by Mrs Harris of Gorringe Park on 7 June 1873. Mr and Mrs Harris donated £3,000 towards the estimated building costs of £4,207 and also gave £1,000 to build the vicarage. The church was consecrated by the Bishop of Winchester on Ascension Day, 14 May 1874. To the left in the lower photograph is Singlegate primary school, erected in 1874 and enlarged in 1897 and again in 1907 for 350 boys, 410 girls and 412 infants. The area in front is covered by watercress beds fed by waters from a small arm of the River Wandle called the Pickle Ditch. The tollgate for the turnpike road stood where Colliers Wood station was built, hence the name Singlegate.

The vicarage of Christ Church, 1913. In 1944 a VI flying bomb fell in Fortescue Road which destroyed six houses, the vicarage and the church hall and severely damaged the church. The church roof had to be replaced, together with the nave ceiling. Restoration was completed in 1953 with stained glass panels in the chancel and west walls.

The Reverend Donald McDonald MA on the vicarage steps, Christ Church, 1913. He was the third vicar at Christ Church and served from 1906 to 1920.

Gorringe Park Avenue, 1912. This row of houses at the northern end of Figge's Marsh had only recently been completed.

Gorringe Park Avenue, *c.* 1930. On the left is the tower of St Barnabas' Church built in 1913–14 and consecrated on 14 November 1914. The houses were built soon after the church was completed. The church cost almost £10,000 to build and could seat 830 people, but remains uncompleted, the north aisle never having been built.

Gorringe Park Avenue, *c*. 1914. Before these houses were erected large crowds would assemble here on bank holidays to watch the pony races along the avenue.

Arthur Odroft's Ironmongers, 58 Gorringe Park Avenue, *c*. 1938. The shop was photographed just before the start of the Second World War and a notice by the entrance states 'Air Raid Precautions – Wanted Volunteers'. Mr Odroft rented out lawnmowers and rollers.

Gorringe Park House, *c.* 1911. The park extended from the large iron gates at Figge's Marsh and another set of gates on the Streatham Road and reached as far as the railway. Mr and Mrs Joseph Wilson were occupants at the time of the photograph and assisted with the building of St Barnabas' Church by selling an acre of land at less than the market price. Later the house was occupied by William and Fanny Harris and after their deaths the house became an orphanage.

Rationing was introduced during the First World War in 1917 and local authorities were persuaded to release open land to be cultivated as allotments to grow fruit and vegetables. Many local inhabitants took up the opportunity and this group of men at Gorringe Park are proudly holding some large marrows they have grown.

The avenue leading up to Gorringe Park House, *c.* 1913. Part of the house was in use as an animal welfare institute at this time. The park was privately owned but not closed off to the public and anyone could use the internal roads. The roads were not well constructed and when building development started shortly before the First World War the roads turned to a sea of mud.

St Barnabas' Church, Gorringe Park, *c.* 1912. The foundation stone of the church hall was laid by Princess Louise Augusta of Schleswig Holstein on 11 July 1908 with the Bishop of Kingston, Doctor Hook, conducting the service. The hall was opened in January 1909 and could seat 500. It was used as the church until 1914 and is still used by the local community. The nearby church was consecrated on 14 November 1914.

Streatham Road, *c.* 1914. Just beyond the person in white on the bicycle is the Roe bridge which carries the road over the River Graveney, the boundary line between London and Surrey and, of course, Wandsworth and Mitcham. The bridge has a stone plaque, reinstated in 1992, that dates from 1652. This commemorated an earlier rebuilding using funds donated in 1542 by John Wilford of the Merchant Tailors Company for the upkeep of Mitcham Lane. John Wilford owned the land that became the Mitcham Manor of Biggin and Tamworth.

The Chestnuts, now called Renshaw Corner, *c.* 1910. This building is opposite Figge's Marsh in Streatham Road and, at the time of the photograph, the firework manufacturer, James Pain & Sons, used it as their head office. The company moved here from Brixton in 1872, and occupied The Chestnuts from 1898 until after the First World War. The company works were at Eastfields, now covered by a council estate. The Georgian house is now privately owned.

A cricket game on Figge's Marsh, 1912. The marsh has been a popular venue for sport for some years and each Sunday is crowded with football teams. The 1987 hurricane brought down many of the trees but the local authority subsequently replaced these.

Figge's Marsh, *c.* 1930.

The allotments on Figge's Marsh, *c.* 1918. The playing fields were sacrificed for vegetable cultivation during the First World War. The area is named after William Figge, who held land in North Mitcham from 1357.

The Swan Inn, London Road, *c.* 1905. This public house dates from about 1808 and in coaching days was frequented by Epsom race-goers, especially on Derby Day. The pub was extended and modified in the 1890s.

Mr and Mrs Richard Kerr, 1904. They are on the balcony of their house, Fairview, no. 4 Sibthorp Terrace on London Road, just along from Swains Road. The photograph was taken by their daughter, Katie Kerr, and the family reproduced it on their own postcards. Mr Kerr was a fellow of the Royal Astronomical Society.

Armfield Crescent, *c.* 1955. This post-Second World War high-rise development was erected by Mitcham Council and located off London Road, near the public library on the right.

Monarch Parade, London Road, *c.* 1950. This row of shops and flats was erected shortly before the start of the Second World War on the site of Holborn Schools. The building has since been totally cement rendered and painted white.

Eagle House, London Road, *c.* 1910. This house dates back to the early eighteenth century and has had various owners. The land was formerly owned by Sir Walter Raleigh. The house became the home of several City bankers and was in use as a school when Merton Council acquired the property. It was left empty for a number of years and then sold off in 1991, when it was renovated for office use.

Church Road, *c.* 1912. On the right is The Bull public house, at no. 32 Church Road, which has records going back to 1780. However, it is thought that this building may date from as early as 1703.

The parish church of St Peter and St Paul, *c.* 1914. The first mention of a church at Mitcham is from about 1170. The thirteenth-century church of flint and stone was added to and extended over the years, but was not considered large enough to cope with the increased population. The church was rebuilt in 1821 with room for 1,100 people.

Church Road, Mitcham, *c.* 1924. F. & M. Sheen's newsagent's and confectioner's shop on the left, at no. 323, appears to act like a magnet to the young children gathered outside. The attraction for the young girl is no doubt the display of dolls in the window. Next door, at no. 325, is the Estate Provision and Grocery Store, run by Mrs C. Coeshill.

The new houses in Western Road, *c.* 1924.

Western Road, *c.* 1906. Nowadays the gas holder is the only reminder of the gas producing plant located here from 1867 to 1960. The plant became a British gas storage facility and gas distribution station in 1960. It is very difficult to visualize this scene today as vitually every structure, except the gas holder, has been demolished.

The Holborn Schools and Union Workhouse, London Road, *c.* 1914. The Poor Law Guardians of St George the Martyr, Southwark bought up land in the Surrey countryside where it proved to be cheaper than in the city. The school, with accommodation for 400 children, was built in 1856 on London Road. The workhouse, behind the school, was built in 1868–70. In 1915 the institution had expanded and held 1,066 inmates and even had its own gas works in Bond Road, managed by a resident engineer, Charles John Rhoades. Several of the workhouse buildings survived as factory premises into the 1950s. But most of the school and workhouse buildings were demolished in about 1934 and Monarch Parade was built on the site (see page 96).

Holborn School band, 1922. Mr J.F. Beeson, bandmaster, is seated in the centre. Only one boy has the pluck to smile; everyone else seems to be taking the occasion very seriously. The band attended many local functions, fêtes and celebrations. This photograph was taken in the grounds of St Benedict's Hospital, Church Lane, Tooting.

Catherine Gladstone Convalescent Home, *c.* 1920. The house was built in 1864 for a railway engineer, George Parker Bidder, and was converted into a convalescent home in 1900. The house was called Ravensbury Park House and actually stood west of the River Wandle in Morden, near Bishopsford Road and Seddon Road. The house was demolished after it was damaged by enemy action during the Second World War.

The Catherine Gladstone Convalescent Home was used as a military hospital during the First World War. The patients were given a bright blue suit and a red tie to wear.

The Gertrude Blaber ward for children at the Catherine Gladstone Convalescent Home, *c.* 1925. The day nursery was well equipped to keep the children's minds and bodies active. The young girl who sent the postcard below had been a patient there in 1925 for eleven weeks and said the children enjoyed themselves so much many did not want to go home.

Catherine Gladstone and her husband William Ewart Gladstone (1809–98), Prime Minister on several occasions, 1868–74, 1880–85, 1886 and 1892–4. Catherine Gladstone founded the convalescent home named after her in 1866.

Patients are wheeled out in their beds to gain some fresh air on the south-east front of the Catherine Gladstone Convalescent Home, *c.* 1925.

The three weatherboarded cottages formerly known as the Flour Mill Houses, *c.* 1910. These buildings are on the banks of the River Wandle near Grove Mill overlooking the Watermeads. The address was 459 London Road.

The River Wandle at Mitcham, *c.* 1914. This view, from Mitcham bridge at Bishopsford Road, is of the Wandle Fisheries at the Watermeads. The Wandle had been famous for trout fishing since the seventeenth century, but with the building of the Beddington Sewage Works fewer trout were spawning in the Wandle. The Wandle fisheries was a project to restock the river, but few trout survived beyond the 1920s. The Crown Mill is on the left and Glover's snuff mill is to the right behind the trees. The National Trust Watermeads property is in the foreground.

Two views of the water splash and bridge over the River Wandle on the road to Sutton, *c.* 1910. The Grove Mill and the Crown Mill were on the left.

Two views of The Surrey Arms public house, Morden Road, *c.* 1905. The early nineteenth-century weatherboarded pub was rebuilt in the 1930s in a mock Tudor style, although on a far larger scale, with three storeys. The taller building in the above view survives.

The road to lower Morden from Mitcham, 1910.

Fishing for tiddlers in the River Wandle, *c.* 1906. These youngsters were trying their luck at the water splash on the Sutton Road, where the London Road meets Bishopsford Road. In the background is the Grove Mill.

A man and his dog negotiate this stile at Ravensbury Park, near the River Wandle, *c.* 1908.

Albert Road, *c.* 1919. This road lies between Commonside West and London Road.

Camomile Avenue, *c*. 1927. To improve housing conditions after the First World War Mitcham UDC built these properties. The cry across the land was 'Homes Fit for Heroes'. Camomile was only one of a host of aromatic plants and herbs fomerly grown in Mitcham. These included rhubarb, liquorice, mint, poppies, peppermint, wormwood, aniseed, lavender and roses.

Caithness Road, *c*. 1914. In 1915 the only trade listed in local directories for this road was Frank Russell, plumber at no. 1. Otto Schröter, a baker, lived at no. 70. His life must have been difficult at this time as the shop windows of many German bakers were being smashed, as happened in Tooting. Many German immigrants anglicized their names during 1914–15.

Biggin Avenue, *c*. 1927. This is situated at the end of Camomile Avenue.

Clarendon Grove, *c*. 1914. This road is not far from Three Kings Pond. The Minion Baptist Chapel was situated here. Only one house was named, no. 13, Sunnyside.

Cranmer Road, *c.* 1910. On the right is the Catholic Church of St Peter and St Paul, completed in 1889 to the designs of the architect, Robert Masters Chart. He also designed the Vestry Hall, next to The Cricketers public house. To the left of the church, nos 3 to 7 survive and nos 3, 4, 5 date from the late eighteenth century. The Wilson Hospital was built just to the left of this row.

Bank Avenue, *c.* 1924. This road lies off Lewis Road, which is to the east of Church Road. Jones' pharmacy is on the left and has now been converted into a private house.

Graham Avenue, *c.* 1914. Fernlea Avenue is at the far end. The Revd Sydney Jackson, chaplain to the Holborn Schools and Workhouse, lived at no. 12, 1913–14. Arthur Edmund Hayes, secretary and subscription agent of the Mitcham Conservative and Unionist Association lived at St Cross, no. 30 Graham Avenue, 1915–16.

Hawthorne Avenue, *c.* 1914. This road lies off Church Road.

Langdale Avenue, *c.* 1914. This road is situated off London Road and leads to the strangely named Cold Blows. The Revd Wallace Perry MA AKC, curate of Mitcham parish church, lived at no. 9. Some of the more extravagant house names were St Breludes, St Leonards and Chamonix.

Madeira Road, *c.* 1933. This road is off Commonside West.

Manor Road, *c.* 1930. At no. 219, on the right, was the United Dairies shop. Rowan Road is to the right and Wide Way is to the left, with Northborough Road behind the cameraman.

Melrose Road, *c.* 1911. The developers were quick to put up the houses but, as in this and other roads within this block, they left the roads as gravel tracks, or on some occasions just a corduroy of railway sleepers. It was left to the local authorities to prepare and maintain a proper surface.

Mitcham Park, *c.* 1914. This unmetalled road was home to the Revd William Kendrick MA, vicar of St Mark's, at no. 11. The Revd John Webster Williams, curate of Mitcham and honorary secretary of Mitcham Park Lawn Tennis and Croquet Club, lived at no. 24.

Oakwood Avenue, *c.* 1924. Harold Thomas' confectioner's shop was at no. 2, on the right. At the far end of the road new houses are in the course of completion.

Tamworth Lane, *c.* 1926. Typke and King Ltd, manufacturing chemists, had premises here. Houses were not numbered before the First World War, but named, for example, Tamworth House and Crowhurst. Frederick Harvey, cow keeper, lived in the road before the First World War. His trade is not now associated with the area.

Park Avenue, off Streatham Road, *c.* 1914. In 1914 Alfred Dean, estate agent, lived at no. 7. William Archelaus Williams LMSSA Lond., physician and surgeon, lived at no. 8.

Vectis Road, *c.* 1920. Before the First World War, when the area was still the Tooting Junction Golf Course, tram drivers in Southcroft Road would describe this tract of land as the prairie. The other road names on the Links Estate follow alphabetically A to J, then jump to Links Road, then Seeley Road and finish with Vectis Road, the Roman name for the Isle of Wight.

Whitford Gardens, *c.* 1914. Alfred C. Melhuish, estate agent, lived at no. 18. Frederick G. Ashwell, gardener, lived at no. 1 and Clement Arnold, chandler, at no. 7.

Sutton Road, *c*. 1912.

Sutton Road, *c*. 1920. The two cyclists have the road entirely to themselves.

Wandle Road, *c.* 1910. A few cows in the field are left undisturbed to chew the cud. The roadway, near what is now Ravensbury Park, has been churned into a sea of mud.

Billy Wood had his motor cycle supply business and works at 472 London Road, Mitcham during the 1930s. His speciality was supplying Velocette motor cycles for which he offered three months' free service if supplied by him. Among the services he offered were decarbonizing and valve grinding (costing 10 *s*), reboring barrels, and supplying Velocette piston rings and gudgeon pins from stock (costing 15*s*). His own Velocette, seen here, was chromium plated throughout.

The Elizabethan pageant on Coronation Day, 22 June 1911. Queen Elizabeth I visited Sir Julius Caesar Adelmere, master of the rolls under James I, in Mitcham in 1598. She also visited Mitcham on four other recorded occasions, and it was decided to recall these visits in the pageant.

Coronation Day procession through Mitcham, 22 June 1911. The procession was gathered outside the clubroom of Mitcham Cricket Club on the cricket green. The horses and wagons seen here were supplied by Camwal & Co., chemists who supplied medical items 'to his majesty's government' and also manufactured a range of aerated drinks.

The clubhouse at Mitcham Golf Club, *c.* 1910. The golf course on the common was laid out in 1891 to the designs of Mr Hibsley Cox. Among some of the early members were parliamentarians such as Lord Balfour. The club was originally named The Princes and was private. Outside pressure forced the club to become public in 1924 and it changed its name to Mitcham Golf Club. The Princes Golf Club now operates from Sandwich in Kent. The old wooden clubhouse burnt down in 1933.

Swans on Three Kings Pond, *c.* 1953. They were a common sight, but since the 1970s they have been overwhelmed by the greater numbers of Canada geese.

The First Mitcham Scout Group, *c.* 1918. It was founded in 1908, the same year that Baden Powell founded the Scout movement. The First Mitcham Scouts met at the Lower Mitcham Schools in Church Road. By 1948 there were twelve groups in Mitcham. Mr Hugh B. Gibbs joined the First Mitcham Scouts in 1909 and by 1948 had become the leader of scouting in Mitcham.

The pupils of Lower Mitcham Infants School, group number six, *c.* 1908.

St Mark's Church, St Mark's Road, seen here soon after completion in 1910. It had space for over 650 people.

Mitcham Wanderers Football Club, 1920–1. The team and committee are seen here with the trophies won that season. They were the winners of the London Junior Cup and the South Western Cup and champions of the Junior Section Southern Suburban League and of the premier division of Thornton Heath League.

Tritton's Corner, *c.* 1910. Rain must have threatened as the policeman is wearing his cape.

Benninga's British margarine factory, Mortimer Road, *c.* 1935. The company produced a range of margarines called Sunniface, Wayside and BBM, which was Butter Blended Margarine. They also supplied their own brand of cooking lard called Lardex, and Vitsu, a shredded beef suet.

The Central School, on Rowan Road near Streatham Park cemetery, *c.* 1933. The school had only recently been built at the time of this photograph and became known as the Rowan County School. It is now known as the Rowan High School for Girls and is also an adult education centre.

The cricket pavilion, on the cricket green at Mitcham, *c.* 1910. The pavilion only dates from earlier this century, when Mitcham Cricket Club transferred from The Cricketers public house. The Cricket Green is to the left behind the cameraman.

BIBLIOGRAPHY

Baker, Revd E., *St Barnabas Church, Mitcham 1914–1939*, 1939

Campion, P., *History of North Mitcham*, (unpublished) 1973

East Mitcham Log, East Mitcham Rate Payers Association, 1938

Goodman, Judith, *Merton and Morden – A Pictorial History*, 1995

Harris, Nick, *Archive Photographs of Mitcham*, 1996

Jowett, Evelyn M., *A History of Merton & Morden*, 1951

Kelly's and Trim's Local Directories

Loobey, P., *Wimbledon in Old Photographs*, 1995

Merton Park – Expanding Suburb 1914–31, John Innes Society, 1986

Merton Park – The Quiet Suburb 1904–14, John Innes Society, 1984

Mitcham – A Historical Glimpse, Merton Libraries, 1988

Mitcham Fair, Merton Libraries, 1991

Mitcham Industries Fair Guide, 1939

Montague, E., *Mitcham, A Brief History*, 1987

Montague, E., *Mitcham, A Pictorial History*, 1991

Montague, E., *Old Mitcham*, 1993

Nutshell History of Merton, Merton Libraries, 1977

Osborn, Helen, *Inn and Around London – Young and Co.'s Pubs*, 1991

The Parish of Christ Church, Mitcham, church leaflet, 1993

Rathbone, Philip, *Paradise Merton*, 1973

Sixty Years of the Northern, London Transport, 1967

Wimbledon Borough News

BRITAIN IN OLD PHOTOGRAPHS

erystwyth & North Ceredigion
ound Abingdon
ton
lerney: A Second Selection
ong the Avon from Stratford to
Tewkesbury
rincham
nersham
ound Amesbury
glesey
nold & Bestwood
nold & Bestwood: A Second
Selection
undel & the Arun Valley
hbourne
ound Ashby-de-la-Zouch
ro Aircraft
lesbury
ham & Tooting
buryshire
nes, Mortlake & Sheen
nsley
h
consfield
dford
dfordshire at Work
dworth
verley
xley
leford
ston
mingham Railways
hop's Stortford &
Sawbridgeworth
hopstone & Seaford
hopstone & Seaford: A Second
Selection
ck Country Aviation
ck Country Railways
ck Country Road Transport
ckburn
ckpool
ound Blandford Forum
tchley
lton
urnemouth
adford
aintree & Bocking at Work
econ
entwood
idgwater & the River Parrett
idlington
idport & the Bride Valley
ierley Hill
ighton & Hove
ighton & Hove: A Second
Selection
istol
ound Bristol
ixton & Norwood
ly Broadstairs & St Peters
omley, Keston & Hayes

Buckingham & District
Burford
Bury
Bushbury
Camberwell
Cambridge
Cannock Yesterday & Today
Canterbury: A Second Selection
Castle Combe to Malmesbury
Chadwell Heath
Chard & Ilminster
Chatham Dockyard
Chatham & Gillingham
Cheadle
Cheam & Belmont
Chelmsford
Cheltenham: A Second Selection
Cheltenham at War
Cheltenham in the 1950s
Chepstow & the River Wye
Chesham Yesterday & Today
Cheshire Railways
Chester
Chippenham & Lacock
Chiswick
Chorley & District
Cirencester
Around Cirencester
Clacton-on-Sea
Around Clitheroe
Clwyd Railways
Clydesdale
Colchester
Colchester 1940–70
Colyton & Seaton
The Cornish Coast
Corsham & Box
The North Cotswolds
Coventry: A Second Selection
Around Coventry
Cowes & East Cowes
Crawley New Town
Around Crawley
Crewkerne & the Ham Stone
Villages
Cromer
Croydon
Crystal Palace, Penge & Anerley
Darlington
Darlington: A Second Selection
Dawlish & Teignmouth
Deal
Derby
Around Devizes
Devon Aerodromes
East Devon at War
Around Didcot & the Hagbournes
Dorchester
Douglas
Dumfries
Dundee at Work
Durham People

Durham at Work
Ealing & Northfields
East Grinstead
East Ham
Eastbourne
Elgin
Eltham
Ely
Enfield
Around Epsom
Esher
Evesham to Bredon
Exeter
Exmouth & Budleigh Salterton
Fairey Aircraft
Falmouth
Farnborough
Farnham: A Second Selection
Fleetwood
Folkestone: A Second Selection
Folkestone: A Third Selection
The Forest of Dean
Frome
Fulham
Galashiels
Garsington
Around Garstang
Around Gillingham
Gloucester
Gloucester: from the Walwin
Collection
North Gloucestershire at War
South Gloucestershire at War
Gosport
Goudhurst to Tenterden
Grantham
Gravesend
Around Gravesham
Around Grays
Great Yarmouth
Great Yarmouth: A Second
Selection
Greenwich & Woolwich
Grimsby
Around Grimsby
Grimsby Docks
Gwynedd Railways
Hackney: A Second Selection
Hackney: A Third Selection
From Haldon to Mid-Dartmoor
Hammersmith & Shepherds Bush
Hampstead to Primrose Hill
Harrow & Pinner
Hastings
Hastings: A Second Selection
Haverfordwest
Hayes & West Drayton
Around Haywards Heath
Around Heathfield
Around Heathfield: A Second
Selection
Around Helston

Around Henley-on-Thames
Herefordshire
Herne Bay
Heywood
The High Weald
The High Weald: A Second
Selection
Around Highworth
Around Highworth & Faringdon
Hitchin
Holderness
Honiton & the Otter Valley
Horsham & District
Houghton-le-Spring &
Hetton-le-Hole
Houghton-le-Spring & Hetton-le-
Hole: A Second Selection
Huddersfield: A Second Selection
Huddersfield: A Third Selection
Ilford
Ilfracombe
Ipswich: A Second Selection
Islington
Jersey: A Third Selection
Kendal
Kensington & Chelsea
East Kent at War
Keswick & the Central Lakes
Around Keynsham & Saltford
The Changing Face of Keynsham
Kingsbridge
Kingston
Kinver
Kirkby & District
Kirkby Lonsdale
Around Kirkham
Knowle & Dorridge
The Lake Counties at Work
Lancashire
The Lancashire Coast
Lancashire North of the Sands
Lancashire Railways
East Lancashire at War
Around Lancaster
Lancing & Sompting
Around Leamington Spa
Around Leamington Spa:
A Second Selection
Leeds in the News
Leeds Road & Rail
Around Leek
Leicester
The Changing Face of Leicester
Leicester at Work
Leicestershire People
Around Leighton Buzzard &
Linslade
Letchworth
Lewes
Lewisham & Deptford:
A Second Selection
Lichfield

Lincoln
Lincoln Cathedral
The Lincolnshire Coast
Liverpool
Around Llandudno
Around Lochaber
Theatrical London
Around Louth
The Lower Fal Estuary
Lowestoft
Luton
Lympne Airfield
Lytham St Annes
Maidenhead
Around Maidenhead
Around Malvern
Manchester
Manchester Road & Rail
Mansfield
Marlborough: A Second Selection
Marylebone & Paddington
Around Matlock
Melton Mowbray
Around Melksham
The Mendips
Merton & Morden
Middlesbrough
Midsomer Norton & Radstock
Around Mildenhall
Milton Keynes
Minehead
Monmouth & the River Wye
The Nadder Valley
Newark
Around Newark
Newbury
Newport, Isle of Wight
The Norfolk Broads
Norfolk at War
North Fylde
North Lambeth
North Walsham & District
Northallerton
Northampton
Around Norwich
Nottingham 1944–74
The Changing Face of Nottingham
Victorian Nottingham
Nottingham Yesterday & Today
Nuneaton
Around Oakham
Ormskirk & District
Otley & District
Oxford: The University
Oxford Yesterday & Today
Oxfordshire Railways: A Second Selection
Oxfordshire at School
Around Padstow
Pattingham & Wombourne
Penwith
Penzance & Newlyn
Around Pershore
Around Plymouth
Poole
Portsmouth
Poulton-le-Fylde
Preston
Prestwich
Pudsey
Radcliffe
RAF Chivenor
RAF Cosford
RAF Hawkinge
RAF Manston
RAF Manston: A Second Selection
RAF St Mawgan
RAF Tangmere
Ramsgate & Thanet Life
Reading
Reading: A Second Selection
Redditch & the Needle District
Redditch: A Second Selection
Richmond, Surrey
Rickmansworth
Around Ripley
The River Soar
Romney Marsh
Romney Marsh: A Second Selection
Rossendale
Around Rotherham
Rugby
Around Rugeley
Ruislip
Around Ryde
St Albans
St Andrews
Salford
Salisbury
Salisbury: A Second Selection
Salisbury: A Third Selection
Around Salisbury
Sandhurst & Crowthorne
Sandown & Shanklin
Sandwich
Scarborough
Scunthorpe
Seaton, Lyme Regis & Axminster
Around Seaton & Sidmouth
Sedgley & District
The Severn Vale
Sherwood Forest
Shrewsbury
Shrewsbury: A Second Selection
Shropshire Railways
Skegness
Around Skegness
Skipton & the Dales
Around Slough
Smethwick
Somerton & Langport
Southampton
Southend-on-Sea
Southport
Southwark
Southwell
Southwold to Aldeburgh
Stafford
Around Stafford
Staffordshire Railways
Around Staveley
Stepney
Stevenage
The History of Stilton Cheese
Stoke-on-Trent
Stoke Newington
Stonehouse to Painswick
Around Stony Stratford
Around Stony Stratford: A Second Selection
Stowmarket
Streatham
Stroud & the Five Valleys
Stroud & the Five Valleys: A Second Selection
Stroud's Golden Valley
The Stroudwater and Thames & Severn Canals
The Stroudwater and Thames & Severn Canals: A Second Selection
Suffolk at Work
Suffolk at Work: A Second Selection
The Heart of Suffolk
Sunderland
Sutton
Swansea
Swindon: A Third Selection
Swindon: A Fifth Selection
Around Tamworth
Taunton
Around Taunton
Teesdale
Teesdale: A Second Selection
Tenbury Wells
Around Tettenhall & Codshall
Tewkesbury & the Vale of Gloucester
Thame to Watlington
Around Thatcham
Around Thirsk
Thornbury to Berkeley
Tipton
Around Tonbridge
Trowbridge
Around Truro
TT Races
Tunbridge Wells
Tunbridge Wells: A Second Selection
Twickenham
Uley, Dursley & Cam
The Upper Fal
The Upper Tywi Valley
Uxbridge, Hillingdon & Cowley
The Vale of Belvoir
The Vale of Conway
Ventnor
Wakefield
Wallingford
Walsall
Waltham Abbey
Wandsworth at War
Wantage, Faringdon & the Vale Villages
Around Warwick
Weardale
Weardale: A Second Selection
Wednesbury
Wells
Welshpool
West Bromwich
West Wight
Weston-super-Mare
Around Weston-super-Mare
Weymouth & Portland
Around Wheatley
Around Whetstone
Whitchurch to Market Drayton
Around Whitstable
Wigton & the Solway Plain
Willesden
Around Wilton
Wimbledon
Around Windsor
Wingham, Addisham & Littlebourne
Wisbech
Witham & District
Witney
Around Witney
The Witney District
Wokingham
Around Woodbridge
Around Woodstock
Woolwich
Woolwich Royal Arsenal
Around Wootton Bassett, Cricklade & Purton
Worcester
Worcester in a Day
Around Worcester
Worcestershire at Work
Around Worthing
Wotton-under-Edge to Chipping Sodbury
Wymondham & Attleborough
The Yorkshire Wolds